WILLIAM THE CONQUEROR

Becomes King of England

History for Kids Books

Children's European History

BABY PROFESSOR

EDUCATION KIDS

Speedy Publishing LLC

40 E. Main St. #1156

Newark, DE 19711

www.speedypublishing.com

In this book, we're going to talk about how William the Conqueror became England's king. So, let's get right to it!

WHO WAS WILLIAM THE CONQUEROR?

In 1066, William the Conqueror landed at Sussex. His goal was to capture the British Isles. He accomplished that goal and eventually became the King of England. He influenced the language, national spirit, and culture and became one of Europe's most important rulers.

Battle Abbey, East Sussex

Robert I

ROBERT-LE-MAGNIFIQUE

EARLY LIFE

William was the son of Robert I and Herleva. She gave birth to him in 1028 AD. His father's rank was the Duke of Normandy and his mother Herleva was the daughter of a craftsman who tanned animal hides for a living. It was said that William's father was enchanted by Herleva when he first saw her from the rooftop of his castle at Falaise.

He watched her washing clothing in the stream near the tannery. Although Robert loved Herleva, he was a noble and she was a humble tanner's daughter so they couldn't marry. Herleva had two children by Robert, William and Adelaide. Even though Robert never married Herleva, his relationship with her elevated her status. He convinced her to marry a knight by the name of Herluin de Conteville, who was his good friend.

William I

King Henry I

In 1034 AD, William's father held a meeting with the important noblemen of his lands and persuaded them to acknowledge William as his heir. He wanted his only son to inherit his position as Duke of Normandy. The French king, King Henry I, the feudal lord of the dukes in that region, agreed to the decision. Content that William would take his place, Robert I left for Jerusalem. On his way traveling home, Robert I died in Nicaea in 1035.

WILLIAM BECOMES THE DUKE OF NORMANDY

Seven-year-old William was immediately crowned with his father's title. However, because he was illegitimate, many nobles believed he shouldn't have been given the position and didn't have the right to take it. There were attempts on his life. Fortunately, William had two protectors. His great-uncle was an archbishop and he took the young William under his wing. After his great-uncle passed away, the king of France, Henry I helped William to keep his position.

Coronation of William the Conqueror

Corfe Castle Isle built by William the Conqueror

THE BATTLE OF VAL-ES-DUNES

In 1047, William's cousin, by the name of Guy of Burgundy, gathered noblemen and troops to fight and defeat William. The two met and their troops attacked each other. This battle was called the Battle of Val-es-Dunes.

William was victorious and it was then that he grabbed power over Normandy. During the next thirteen years William tried to gather his forces together to make his power strong in the region. He was able to fight back when Geoffrey Martel tried to grab power. The men would eventually fight on the same side. By 1060, Normandy was firmly under William's control.

DOOMS
-DAY

BOOK

William I, Lichfield Cathedral

Queen Matilda and Her Tapestry

MARRIAGE TO MATILDA OF FLANDERS

William joined in marriage with Matilda who lived in Flanders in 1050 AD. The purpose of the marriage was to join William and the duchy of Flanders. A duchy is a vast region ruled by a duke.

THE INVASION OF ENGLAND

Sixteen years after William's marriage, the King of England, who was Edward the Confessor, passed away. William was in Edward's bloodline through his uncle. He announced that Edward had promised he would have the throne. Others had intentions for the throne as well. The citizens wanted Harold Godwinson, a very powerful and wealthy noble, to be crowned king.

Edward the Confessor

King Harold II

They crowned him in 1066, but his rule didn't last long. King Edward had just died the day before the coronation. In the meantime, Norway's King Hardrada decided that he wanted to claim the English crown for his own. Hardrada overran England. Moving forward, King Harold II went to do battle with the invader. With his two competitors fighting, William seized the opportunity. He traveled across the English Channel with his army and made camp near Hastings.

WILLIAM AGAINST HAROLD

King Harold II was victorious against the invaders from Norway, but now he was faced with doing battle with William and his troops. William had gathered men from all different countries of Europe. To get them to enlist, he had promised them land in England as soon as he was crowned king. William's archers and knights were armed and on horseback. Harold's soldiers were on foot and couldn't win against William's superior army. William and his troops were victorious and Harold was killed.

The Battle of Hastings

William after the Battle of Hastings

BECOMING KING

William and his troops soon attacked and captured London. William had conquered all of England and was crowned as the country's king. He ruled for twenty-one years between 1066-1087 AD.

REVOLTS IN NORTHERN ENGLAND

Not everyone was happy that William was king. He was entangled in the first few years by revolts organized by the people. He became so furious that at one point he ordered his army to burn farms, food, and livestock across the northern part of England. This attack was called the "Harrying of the North." Over 100,000 people were killed by his troops.

King William I

ENTRY

White Tower

ENGLISH CASTLES

In order to show his power, William had castles built throughout England. Two of the most famous of these castles are the White Tower and Windsor Castle, which is located about 22 miles distance from London. Windsor Castle has been used by the British Royalty for over 900 years.

A HUGE SURVEY

In 1085 AD, William commanded that a complete list of all property in England, including land, livestock, and farm equipment be put together. The purpose was to collect taxes from the citizens. At the time, the population of the country wasn't pleased about this. However, today the book sheds a lot of light on the time period and is considered to be a national treasure.

Windsor Castle

WILLIAM THE CONQUEROR'S DEATH

William passed away in 1087 after an accident with his horse while he was fighting in the north of France. His oldest son with Matilda who was named Robert became the Duke of Normandy. His second son named after him became one of the kings of England.

FASCINATING FACTS ABOUT WILLIAM

William was descended from Vikings. He came from the bloodline of Rollo, a famous Viking who raided France in the late ninth century. Eventually, Rollo was given the land of Normandy by a Frankish king to keep the peace and Normandy was where William was born.

Rollo

Battle of Hastings

Because he was illegitimate, William was given the name "William the Bastard." Even after he was a conquering hero and was victorious in battle against the British in the Battle of Hastings he couldn't live it down.

William wanted to marry Matilda of Flanders. She was the granddaughter of Robert II, the King of France. She didn't want to marry him, possibly because of the nature of his birth. William didn't take her rejection lightly. He pulled her off a horse by her long braids. She eventually said yes to marrying him although they must have made a strange couple.

Robert II

William was 6 feet tall and Matilda was only 4 feet 2 inches tall. Although theirs wasn't originally a love match, their marriage was happy and they had 10 children together. He went into an intense depression when she passed away. Unlike other kings during this era, it was thought that through their many years of marriage, William was faithful to his wife.

Legend has it that during William's attack on Alençon, the citizens there mocked him by hanging animal hides to insult his bloodline because his grandfather on his mother's side had been a tanner. To uphold his mother's honor, he had the hands and feet cut off those who had hung up the hides.

William the Conqueror invades England

William couldn't read or write. He spoke French and despite all his efforts he couldn't learn how to speak English. After he conquered England, the members of his court had to speak French and this changed the English Language as new French words blended in.

William had a court jester who rode with him into battle. His job was to lift the spirits of the troops by singing heroic songs about them. When they reached the battle line in England, he pulled out his sword and made fun of the soldiers. He was quickly killed by the English soldiers and this is how the Battle of Hastings started.

Battle of Hastings

William was in good physical shape when he was younger, but as he got older he became very fat. He was sensitive about it and devised a "diet" where he wouldn't consume any food, just drink wine and other alcoholic beverages. The diet didn't work.

William was critically injured during a battle in 1087. When his horse went up on its back legs, he was somehow thrown so hard against his saddle that his intestines ruptured. Over the weeks that followed, his intestines became infected and he died.

William the Conqueror on Horseback

William The Conqueror

About 25% of the population of England is related to the bloodline of William. Many Americans are as well since they have British ancestors.

The name William became really widespread in England after William took power. By the 1200s it had become one of the most common English names for men. It's still ranked in the top 10 names.

Castle of William the Conqueror

Even when he was the ruler of all of England, William chose to live in Normandy.

Awesome! Now you know more about the life of William the Conqueror. You can find more European History books from Baby Professor by searching the website of your favorite book retailer.

Old Jerusalem

Visit

BABY PROFESSOR
EDUCATION KIDS

www.BabyProfessorBooks.com

to download Free Baby Professor eBooks
and view our catalog of new and exciting
Children's Books

Made in the USA
Las Vegas, NV
07 March 2023

68695869R00040